# SUNKEN TREASURE

## by Dee Phillips

**Gareth Stevens Publishing**
A WORLD ALMANAC EDUCATION GROUP COMPANY

Please visit our web site at: www.garethstevens.com
For a free color catalog describing Gareth Stevens Publishing's
list of high-quality books and multimedia programs,
call 1-800-542-2595 (USA) or 1-800-387-3178 (Canada).
Gareth Stevens Publishing's fax: (414) 332-3567.

Library of Congress Cataloging-in-Publication Data available upon request from publisher.
Fax (414) 336-0157 for the attention of the Publishing Records Department.

ISBN 0-8368-3743-6

This North American edition first published in 2004 by
**Gareth Stevens Publishing**
A World Almanac Education Group Company
330 West Olive Street, Suite 100
Milwaukee, WI 53212 USA

This U.S. edition copyright © 2004 by Gareth Stevens, Inc. Original edition copyright © 2003 ticktock
Entertainment Ltd. First published in Great Britain in 2003 by ticktock Media Ltd., Unit 2, Orchard Business
Centre, North Farm Road, Tunbridge Wells, Kent, TN2 3XF. Additional end matter copyright © 2004 by
Gareth Stevens, Inc.

We would like to thank: David Gillingwater, Thorsten Opper at The British Museum, Martin Dean, Director
of the Archaeological Diving Unit at the University of St. Andrews, Scotland, and Elizabeth Wiggans.

Gareth Stevens editor: Carol Ryback
Gareth Stevens cover design: Katherine A. Goedheer

Photo credits:
t=top, b=bottom, c=center, l=left, r=right, OFC=outside front cover, OBC=outside back cover
Alamy: 3bl, 11br, 12b, 13br, 14tr, 15c, 17cr, 28-29, 29tr. John Alston: 4bl. Corbis: 5c, 6tr, 7tr, 7cl, 12cr,
13bl, 15tr, 16-17, 17tr, 19tl, 21cr, 24-25. Mike Dixon/Mountain camera: 8-9. Bob Dunn (courtesy of
the "Kyrenia Ship Project"): 14cr. Heritage Image Collection: 6c, 7tl. Constantinos Ioannou ("Kyrenia-
Liberty" replica): 26-27tc, 27tr, 28tr. Michael Katzev (courtesy of the "Kyrenia Ship Project"): 19tc.

Every effort has been made to trace the copyright holders, and we apologize in advance for any
unintentional omissions. We would be pleased to insert the appropriate acknowledgments in any
subsequent edition of this publication.

Printed in Hong Kong

1 2 3 4 5 6 7 8 9 07 06 05 04 03

Would you like to join an exciting expedition to Greece?

The characters accompanying you — Alex Spencer, Dr. Helen Jones, and Dr. Ioannes Papadimas — are fictitious, but the facts about museums, archaeologists, and scientists represent an accurate view of their work. The ancient Greek shipwreck that you will help to excavate is also fictitious, but the characteristics of the shipwreck and details about life in ancient Greece are based on actual discoveries made by archaeologists.

Can't wait to learn more? Ready to dive for ancient clues?

Then welcome to the City Museum...

# CONTENTS

## CITY MUSEUM PASS

**Name:** Dr. Helen Jones
**Position:** Curator
**Department:** Ancient Greek and Roman Antiquities

**Interests:** Ancient civilizations, digging, travel, and scuba diving.

## CITY MUSEUM PASS

**Name:** Alex Spencer
**Position:** Research assistant
**Department:** Ancient Greek and Roman Antiquities

**Interests:** Ancient history, scuba diving, and computers.

TEMPORARY

# A NEW EXHIBITION

## Day 1

When I volunteered to help out at the City Museum during spring break, I didn't realize what I was getting myself into! I'm a temporary research assistant in the department of ancient Greek and Roman antiquities. The curator of this department and my boss, Dr. Helen Jones, is setting up a new exhibition featuring life in ancient Greece. Dr. Jones says that this ancient civilization is fascinating to study because it influences many aspects of our lives today.

Although I've visited the museum many times, I didn't realize that so much work went on behind the scenes. Curators, architects, scientists, and fund-raisers have all been working for months to prepare for the new exhibition. This morning while I unpacked boxes of items from the storeroom, Dr. Jones checked the crates of precious artifacts that arrived – on loan – from famous museums around the world!

**ANCIENT GREEK POTTERY**
Many decorated pots and vases, like this *amphora* (storage jar), survive today. The detailed designs show scenes from Greek mythology and everyday life in ancient Greece.

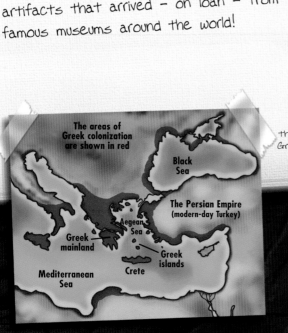

Map of the ancient Greek world.

The areas of Greek colonization are shown in red

Black Sea

The Persian Empire (modern-day Turkey)

Aegean Sea

Greek mainland

Greek islands

Crete

Mediterranean Sea

**THE THEATER**
The ancient Greeks loved the theater. The actors (who were always men) wore masks with exaggerated features to indicate which character they were playing. Masks made it easier for people at the back of the theater to see the actors.

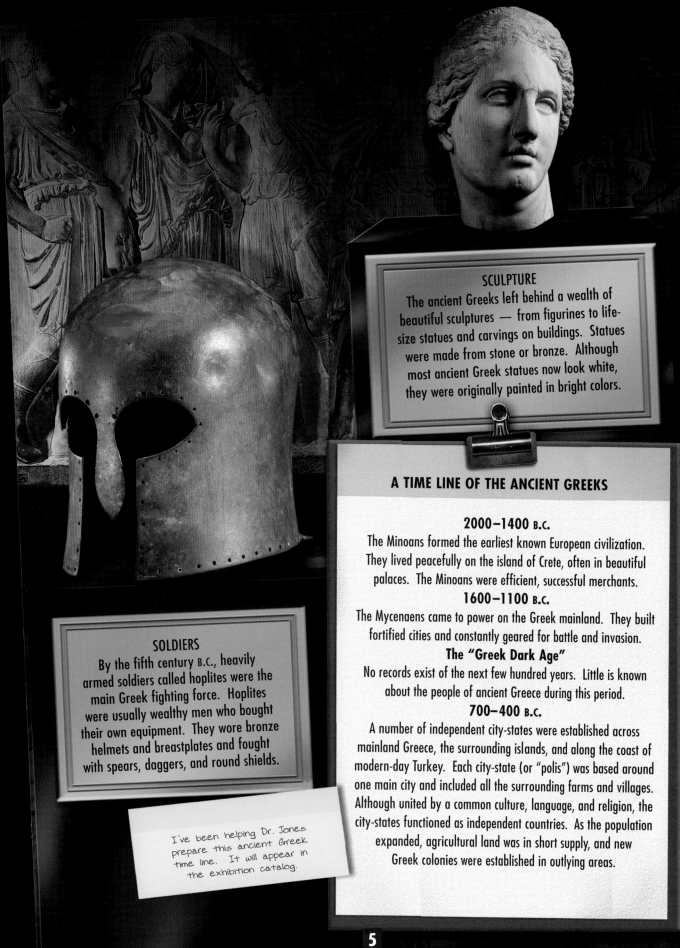

## SCULPTURE

The ancient Greeks left behind a wealth of beautiful sculptures — from figurines to life-size statues and carvings on buildings. Statues were made from stone or bronze. Although most ancient Greek statues now look white, they were originally painted in bright colors.

## A TIME LINE OF THE ANCIENT GREEKS

### 2000–1400 B.C.

The Minoans formed the earliest known European civilization. They lived peacefully on the island of Crete, often in beautiful palaces. The Minoans were efficient, successful merchants.

### 1600–1100 B.C.

The Mycenaens came to power on the Greek mainland. They built fortified cities and constantly geared for battle and invasion.

### The "Greek Dark Age"

No records exist of the next few hundred years. Little is known about the people of ancient Greece during this period.

### 700–400 B.C.

A number of independent city-states were established across mainland Greece, the surrounding islands, and along the coast of modern-day Turkey. Each city-state (or "polis") was based around one main city and included all the surrounding farms and villages. Although united by a common culture, language, and religion, the city-states functioned as independent countries. As the population expanded, agricultural land was in short supply, and new Greek colonies were established in outlying areas.

## SOLDIERS

By the fifth century B.C., heavily armed soldiers called hoplites were the main Greek fighting force. Hoplites were usually wealthy men who bought their own equipment. They wore bronze helmets and breastplates and fought with spears, daggers, and round shields.

I've been helping Dr. Jones prepare this ancient Greek time line. It will appear in the exhibition catalog.

## Day 2

Dr. Jones's specialty is ancient Greek jewelry and fashion. The Greeks wore very simple clothing. Men and women alike wore a linen or wool tunic, topped with a woolen cloak during colder weather. Most Greeks chose to go barefoot or wore leather sandals. Ready-made clothes and fabric were sold in the <u>agora</u> (marketplace), but most people wore homemade clothes. Every ancient Greek girl learned how to weave so that she could produce all the fabric needed to clothe her family.

The jewelry for the exhibition is being unpacked, checked, and cleaned by the museum's conservation department. Many of the pieces have been in storage for years. Among these cartons was a tiny unmarked box that contained a single gold earring, some shells, and what looked like a little map. Dr. Jones is very excited. She thinks the earring dates back to about 400 B.C. Although the ancient Greeks were master craftspeople, gold was in short supply during this period, and very little jewelry was made. This earring could be very rare!

Headbands (diadems) made of ribbons, beads, and gold were a Greek fashion rage. This gold diadem dates back to 300 B.C. Long hair was plaited (braided) and piled high on the head.

Study of ancient Greece: summer 1890

No one knows how the museum acquired the earring. Perhaps someone brought it back from an expedition. Maybe the map pinpoints where the earring was found!

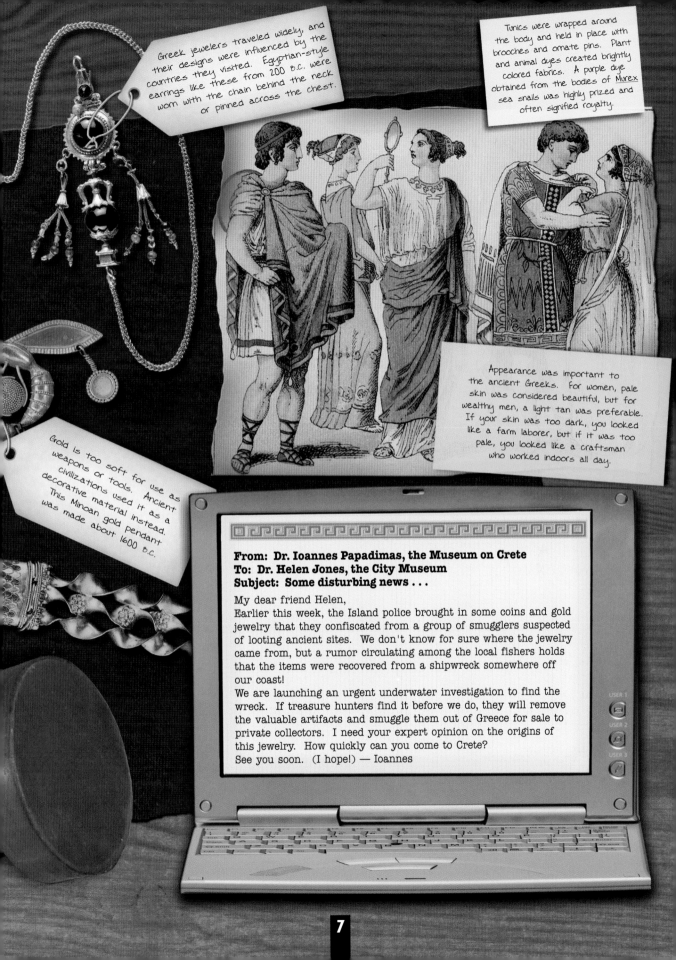

Greek jewelers traveled widely, and their designs were influenced by the countries they visited. Egyptian-style earrings like these from 200 B.C. were worn with the chain behind the neck or pinned across the chest.

Tunics were wrapped around the body and held in place with brooches and ornate pins. Plant and animal dyes created brightly colored fabrics. A purple dye obtained from the bodies of Murex sea snails was highly prized and often signified royalty.

Appearance was important to the ancient Greeks. For women, pale skin was considered beautiful, but for wealthy men, a light tan was preferable. If your skin was too dark, you looked like a farm laborer, but if it was too pale, you looked like a craftsman who worked indoors all day.

Gold is too soft for use as weapons or tools. Ancient civilizations used it as a decorative material instead. This Minoan gold pendant was made about 1600 B.C.

**From: Dr. Ioannes Papadimas, the Museum on Crete**
**To: Dr. Helen Jones, the City Museum**
**Subject: Some disturbing news . . .**

My dear friend Helen,

Earlier this week, the Island police brought in some coins and gold jewelry that they confiscated from a group of smugglers suspected of looting ancient sites. We don't know for sure where the jewelry came from, but a rumor circulating among the local fishers holds that the items were recovered from a shipwreck somewhere off our coast!

We are launching an urgent underwater investigation to find the wreck. If treasure hunters find it before we do, they will remove the valuable artifacts and smuggle them out of Greece for sale to private collectors. I need your expert opinion on the origins of this jewelry. How quickly can you come to Crete?

See you soon. (I hope!) — Ioannes

USER 1
USER 2
USER 3

## Day 5

Dr. Jones asked me to travel with her to the Island of Crete! I barely had time to throw some shorts, T-shirts, and sunglasses into a backpack before we left. Costas, one of Dr. Jones's old friends, met us at the airport in Athens (the capital of Greece) — with his helicopter! We are about to get a bird's-eye view of Greece.

We just flew over Mount Olympus, the legendary home of the Greek gods. From the top of Mount Olympus, these gods watched over the lives of the ordinary people below. But the ancient Greeks also believed their gods behaved like humans. Some were wise, loving, and heroic, while others had faults and made mistakes. The gods fell in love, got married, argued, and even cheated on their husbands and wives! Ancient Greek religion had no moral code. Instead, you simply kept the gods happy, or they would punish you. The best way to find favor with the gods was to visit a temple and sacrifice an animal or to make an offering of silver or gold.

### THE OLYMPICS RETURN TO GREECE

One way to honor the gods was to hold sporting contests. The most famous of these were the Olympic Games. The first Olympics were held at a place called Olympia in 776 B.C. From then on, the Games took place every four years. For five days, men from across the Greek world competed in events such as running, chariot racing, wrestling, boxing, discus, javelin, and long jump. In A.D. 393, the games ceased, but hundreds of years later, the discovery of the ruins of Olympia inspired their revival. In 1896, the first "modern" games were held in Athens. Countries around the world now take turns hosting the Olympics. The Games returned to Athens for the XXVIII Olympiad in 2004.

At 9,570 feet (2,917 meters), Mount Olympus is Greece's tallest mountain.

## Advice from the gods

Ancient Greeks visited an oracle for advice about the future. The most famous oracle was at Delphi on Mount Parnassus, the home of the god Apollo for nine months of the year. Visitors came from across the Greek world to seek Apollo's help by asking questions of the high priestess, "Pythia." The mountain mist helped Pythia fall into a trance and communicate with Apollo. She gave all her answers in riddles. Priests at the temple interpreted the riddles for the visitors.

The ruins of Apollo's temple at Delphi

## Know your Greek gods

**ZEUS:** King of the gods. God of justice, law, morals, and thunder and lightning.

**HERA:** Wife of Zeus. Goddess of women, marriage, and mothers.

**APHRODITE:** Goddess of love, beauty, and fertility.

**APOLLO:** God of music, light, healing, archery, farming, and prophecy.

**DEMETER:** Goddess of grain, crops, and farming.

**DIONYSUS:** God of grapes, wine, and pleasure.

**HEPHAESTUS:** God of fire and metalworking.

**POSEIDON:** The god of the sea, water, horses, and earthquakes.

Clouds often shroud Mount Olympus. The ancient Greeks believed that the clouds gave the gods privacy.

Athena — Zeus's daughter and the goddess of cities, war, and wisdom — was the patron of Athens, for whom the city was named.

## Later that day

Athens is the largest city in Greece. The Acropolis, built on Athens's highest hill, dominates the city. Ancient Greeks built temples and stored treasures safely inside this fortified enclosure. Dr. Jones says the Greek style of architecture has influenced designers and builders throughout history. In fact, even the City Museum's tall stone columns and marble carvings at its main entrance show the Greek influence. Although government buildings and temples were grand and ornate, Greek houses were built simply, with few differences between the homes of the rich and the poor. Homes of rich people were just bigger!

We left Athens after our sightseeing tour. Below us, the rugged, mountainous Greek landscape turned to coastline. In ancient times, traveling by boat around the coast was easier than traveling cross-country over the mountains. As our helicopter flew from mainland Greece toward the island of Crete, I appreciated our modern method of travel!

Ancient Greeks built homes from dried mud bricks painted white to deflect the hot sun, just like modern-day Greek buildings. Most had stone floors, tiled roofs, and a small courtyard.

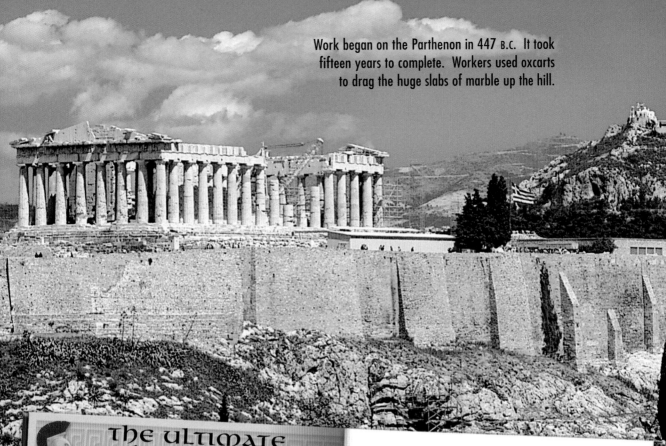

Work began on the Parthenon in 447 B.C. It took fifteen years to complete. Workers used oxcarts to drag the huge slabs of marble up the hill.

# The Ultimate Guide to Greece

## The Athens Acropolis: The Parthenon

At the highest point of the Acropolis is the temple of the Parthenon, dedicated to the goddess Athena. A dramatic frieze (a horizontal, sculptured band) carved into the temple shows scenes of the Athenians holding a great procession in honor of Athena.

## The Theater at Epidaurus

Don't miss visiting the well-preserved, magnificent Theater at Epidaurus, located just a few hours from Athens. Cut into the hillside, its huge, semicircular auditorium amplifies sound to provide all 20,000 spectators with excellent seats. Ancient, day-long performances included tragedies (sad, violent tales of love, war, and old myths) and comedies (plays that made fun of politics, religion, and important local people). Tourists still visit to view performances.

## The Erechtheion

This smaller temple features a famous porch with caryatids (marble statues of women) instead of columns holding up the roof.

# A TRIP TO CRETE

## Day 6

First thing this morning, Dr. Jones and I met with Dr. Papadimas at the island museum. I asked him for the latest information on the shipwreck. So far, the museum's search team was unsuccessful.

When underwater archaeologists explore an ancient shipwreck, they carefully document and record all the objects and their positions. If looters or scavengers get to a site first, they destroy vital clues to the story behind the wreck as they remove anything of value. Accidental damage from fishing nets or visits by curious scuba divers also affect the information offered by an intact shipwreck.

Meanwhile, Dr. Jones confirmed that the items recovered by the police dated to the fifth century B.C., just like the earring from the City Museum. When Dr. Papadimas looked at the map found with the earring, he instantly recognized the area and exclaimed, "It's the Chania lighthouse in the harbor!"

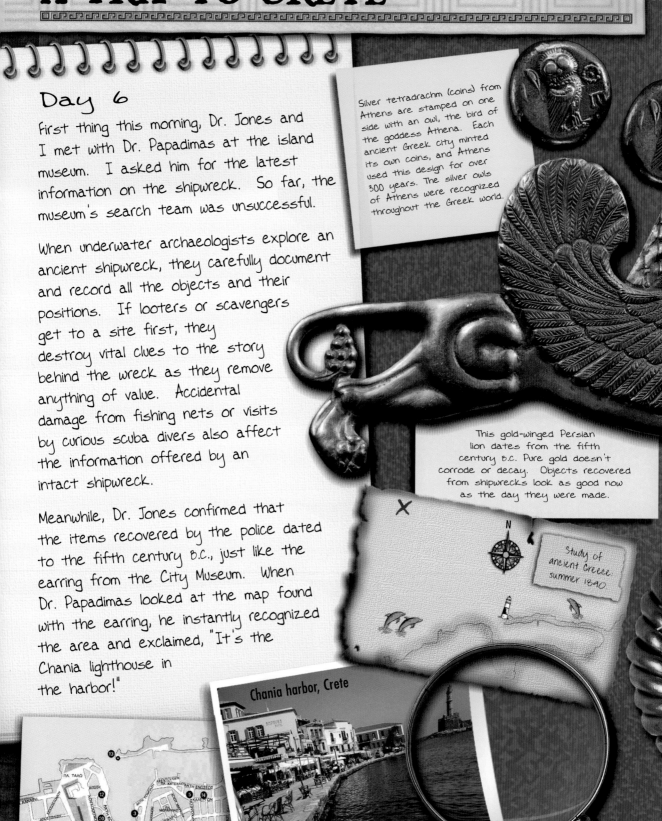

Silver tetradrachm (coins) from Athens are stamped on one side with an owl, the bird of the goddess Athena. Each ancient Greek city minted its own coins, and Athens used this design for over 300 years. The silver owls of Athens were recognized throughout the Greek world.

This gold-winged Persian lion dates from the fifth century B.C. Pure gold doesn't corrode or decay. Objects recovered from shipwrecks look as good now as the day they were made.

Study of ancient Greece: summer 1890.

Chania harbor, Crete

## THESEUS & THE MINOTAUR

Every nine years, King Minos of Crete demanded that seven young men and seven young women sail from Athens to Crete to be fed to the Minotaur. This terrifying monster had the body of a huge, strong man and the head of an angry bull. The Minotaur lived deep within a maze of twisting tunnels called the labyrinth. No one who entered the labyrinth ever returned. One year, a brave young Athenian named Theseus was among those chosen for sacrifice to the Minotaur. But the handsome Theseus charmed King Minos's daughter, Ariadne. She decided to help Theseus. When everyone else was asleep, Ariadne took Theseus to the labyrinth. She gave him a ball of thread and a sword. Ariadne told Theseus to unwind the thread as he walked into the labyrinth. He found the Minotaur in its lair and killed it with the sword. Then Theseus followed the thread out of the labyrinth. He escaped from Crete and returned to Athens as a hero.

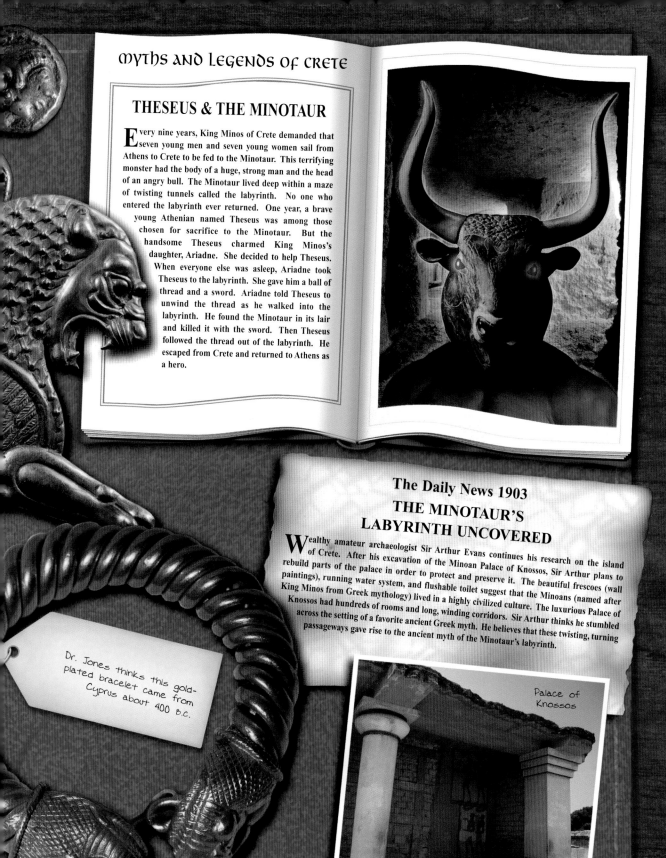

Dr. Jones thinks this gold-plated bracelet came from Cyprus about 400 B.C.

## The Daily News 1903
## THE MINOTAUR'S LABYRINTH UNCOVERED

Wealthy amateur archaeologist Sir Arthur Evans continues his research on the island of Crete. After his excavation of the Minoan Palace of Knossos, Sir Arthur plans to rebuild parts of the palace in order to protect and preserve it. The beautiful frescoes (wall paintings), running water system, and flushable toilet suggest that the Minoans (named after King Minos from Greek mythology) lived in a highly civilized culture. The luxurious Palace of Knossos had hundreds of rooms and long, winding corridors. Sir Arthur thinks he stumbled across the setting of a favorite ancient Greek myth. He believes that these twisting, turning passageways gave rise to the ancient myth of the Minotaur's labyrinth.

Palace of Knossos

## Day 8

Success at last! The museum's divers located the shipwreck site about 1.25 miles (2 km) out of the harbor at about a depth of 100 feet (30 m).

We sailed to the site, which the research divers marked with a buoy. We tied our boat to the buoy to avoid dropping an anchor and destroying any submerged objects or marine life. Dr. Jones said I can dive on the shipwreck because I earned my scuba-diving certification last year. Too cool!

Dr. Jones will be my "dive buddy." We checked our own and then each other's scuba gear and practiced some hand signals for use underwater. Then we entered the water by flipping backwards off the boat. We descended slowly into the warm, blue world and its increasing water pressure.

After about two minutes, Dr. Jones motioned to me. I looked to where she was pointing, and there, far below us, I saw divers working alongside a heap of <u>amphoras</u> (large pottery jars). We were right above the wreck!

A wetsuit allows a layer of water to leak in next to the diver's skin. Body heat warms the trapped water and keeps the diver comfortable.

Lights help divers peer under ledges or into cracks and crevices. It also lets them see the true colors of underwater objects.

A squirrelfish finned in and out of the stack of amphoras.

Most divers carry a dive knife as a safety precaution in case they become tangled in fishing line or a net.

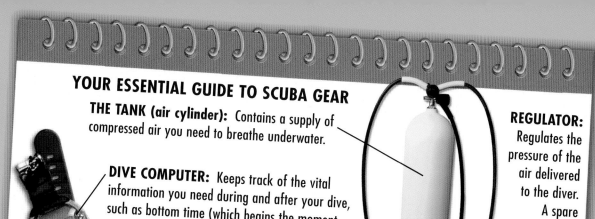

## YOUR ESSENTIAL GUIDE TO SCUBA GEAR

**THE TANK (air cylinder):** Contains a supply of compressed air you need to breathe underwater.

**DIVE COMPUTER:** Keeps track of the vital information you need during and after your dive, such as bottom time (which begins the moment you start your descent and begin breathing compressed air), depth, and water temperature.

**REGULATOR:** Regulates the pressure of the air delivered to the diver. A spare regulator is called an "octopus."

A buoyancy compensator (BC) carries the air tank and contains an air bladder attached to the tank. The diver adjusts the amount of air in the BC to achieve neutral buoyancy underwater. Some BCs have pockets that hold weights so the diver doesn't need to wear a weight belt.

## Two months later

As soon as Dr. Jones and Dr. Papadimas saw the wreck, they confirmed that it was about 2,000 years old. If the jewelry originated from this wreck, we could only imagine what still lay under the thick blanket of muddy sand. Dr. Papadimas began planning the underwater excavation.

Dr. Jones and I returned to Crete after two months at home. As we sailed to the site, Dr. Papadimas explained that a huge team of experts and volunteers was already excavating the wreck. The team includes twenty divers (ten of whom are archaeologists). Other workers tend the salvage boat or catalog the recovered artifacts brought back to the museum.

Underwater archaeologists must work quickly but methodically. Each artifact is measured, numbered, and photographed.

Sometimes a piece of sponge gets caught on dive gear. Sponges live on the seabed. They filter particles of food from the water.

Divers use plastic slates (like this) and pencils to write underwater.

The team cleared a thick layer of tangled seaweed from the site before starting work. They also removed extra sand and debris covering the site using soft jets of water. A suction tube (a type of underwater vacuum cleaner) removes more of the loose material.

Researchers direct the vacuum pumps to flush some of the matter away from the site. They pump other material up to the deck of the boat in order to filter it for artifacts or anything of interest.

Workers build a giant 3-D grid, made of metal and PVC tubing, over the wreck. Archaeologists reference the grid numbers to record the position of each item found at the site.

Metal baskets carry small items to the boat after all the data is recorded. Air bags attached to larger, heavier objects lift them to the surface.

Divers work in pairs for safety. Five pairs go down at a time. At this depth — 100 feet (30 m) — they can only dive twice a day for about 20 minutes each time.

A huge moray eel lives under a rock ledge alongside the wreck. Morays can grow to about 10 feet (3 m) long. They have poor eyesight but very sharp teeth!

An amazing variety of sea life, such as octopuses, squid, crabs, shrimp, sponges, sea anemones, and red and yellow gorgonians (a type of soft coral), lives near the wreck.

## A merchant ship

The team of underwater archaeologists worked hard all summer. Every night, the salvage boat returned with a new batch of artifacts for the museum. After soaking in seawater for thousands of years, items such as clay pots need special handling. Repeated soaks in frequent changes of freshwater removes centuries of sea salt from the artifacts.

As we watched a video of the salvage operation, an octopus scampered across the wreck! I guess enough of the original timber and cargo survived to provide a home for this creature — and to let us identify it as a small cargo vessel. I asked Dr. Papadimas how the wood survived over all that time. He explained that submerged wooden ships deteriorate quickly at first, but then the process slows down. Deep, sand-covered shipwrecks are stable for thousands of years. A fierce storm that churned up the water and shifted the sand probably exposed our ship. Dr. Papadimas clicked to another place on the screen and showed me all our latest finds — a merchant's ship full of sunken treasure!

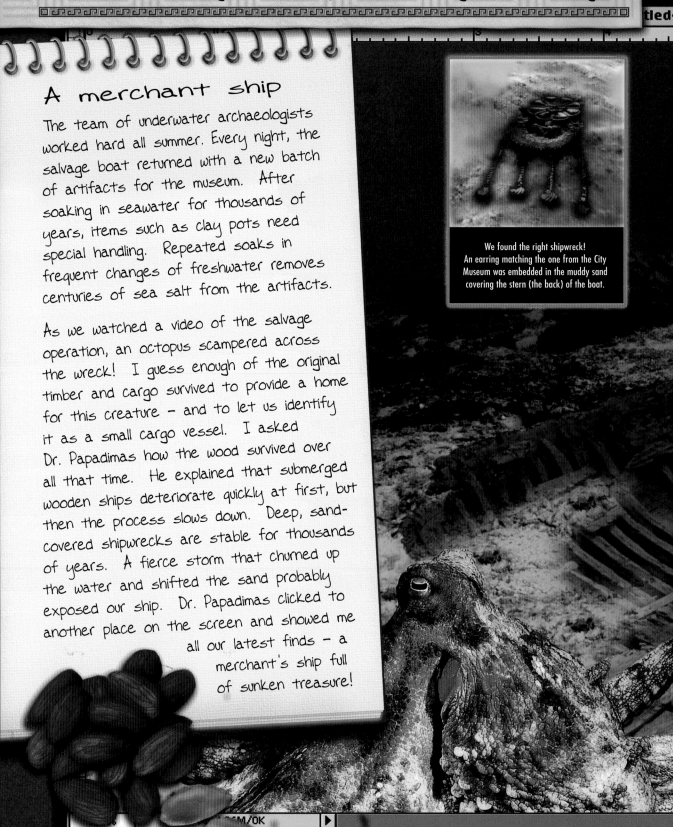

We found the right shipwreck! An earring matching the one from the City Museum was embedded in the muddy sand covering the stern (the back) of the boat.

This gold rhyton (an ornate drinking cup) was used at men-only drinking-and-talking parties called symposiums. We think the Greeks passed the rhyton around until it was empty.

Octopuses found homes in many of the 350 *amphoras* (all-purpose shipping containers of ancient Greece) found on our shipwreck.

We discovered thousands of almonds inside the *amphoras*. Greeks usually transported almonds in sacks, so we think the octopuses carried the almonds into the *amphoras*!

**From: Alex Spencer**
**To: The department of ancient Greek antiquities, the City Museum**
**Subject: Excavation update**

Hi to everyone,

Here's an update — Dr. Papadimas just received confirmation of his funding for raising the wreck! They plan to lift the boat in sections using air bags. The salvage boat will take the sections ashore. The archaeologists are making detailed diagrams of where every piece of timber fits into the ship. Before anything is moved, each piece is numbered, measured, and photographed from every angle. The waterlogged wood will require extensive conservation treatment. (Some of the timbers are the consistency of wet bread.) I wonder how it will smell? — Alex

# THE LAST VOYAGE

## Detective work

When I returned from Crete, I headed straight for the City Museum, where work was underway to discover as much as possible about the ship and its cargo. Dr. Jones says that each voyage would last for several months. Back then, sailors had few instruments and navigated using the stars. Ancient Greek sailors kept land in sight at all times, which is why the ship was found so close to the coast. Our merchant probably bought and sold any type of cargo that was profitable. Crops that thrived in the poor-quality Greek soil, such as olives, were exported, while wood (for shipbuilding) and crops such as grain, that were difficult to grow in Greece, were among the imported cargo.

Dr. Jones brought back some pieces of wood from the ship's hull and some of the almonds. Using a technique called radiocarbon dating, we hope to determine the age of the ship when it sank and possibly when the shipwreck tragedy occurred.

A shipwreck is like an underwater time capsule. By studying all the items found at the wreck site and the items confiscated from the smugglers, we figured out the route the ship followed on its final journey. I used red dots to mark the possible route of the merchant's last voyage on this map.

The silver coins came from Athens. Perhaps the ship sailed from the main port of Piraeus.

**Port of Piraeus, Athens**

The wreck site

**Chania harbor**

Hippopotamus teeth found on the ship were probably from Egypt, where hippos were hunted on the Nile River.

This piece of wood is from the hull of the sunken ship.

## ARCHAEOLOGY TODAY
## EXPLAINING RADIOCARBON DATING

Radiocarbon dating (also called carbon-14 dating) is a reliable scientific method used for determining the age of a once-living organism. Plants absorb an isotope (C-14) of carbon from the air during photosynthesis, and people and animals absorb C-14 when they eat and breathe. When a living thing dies, it stops taking in any new carbon, and the existing isotope inside the organism begins to decay. Scientists know the exact rate at which C-14 decays, and from that they can determine the age of the organism by how much of the C-14 isotope is left.

Our gold lion artifact probably came from the area labeled here as the Persian Empire.

An ancient Greek perfume bottle is in the City Museum's collection. The ancient Greeks made perfumes from flowers and herbs. They also liked imported Persian scents.

Dr. Jones says the design of the <u>amphoras</u> was popular on Rhodes. The jars contain traces of resin for sealing the jars and stopping leaks, which indicates these <u>amphora</u> were used for carrying liquids, such as wine or olive oil.

**Persian Empire**

**Cyprus**

**Rhodes**

**Crete**

**Egypt**

The almonds found on the wreck were probably grown on the island of Cyprus. The gold bracelet was also identified as originating on Cyprus.

**From: Dr. Bob Archer, City Laboratories**
**To: Dr. Helen Jones, the City Museum**
**Subject: Results of radiocarbon dating tests on shipwreck wood and almonds**

Dear Dr. Jones,
The tests on the timber from the shipwreck indicate a radiocarbon date range of 448 to 402 B.C. The radiocarbon dating of the four almonds recovered from the wreck give a date range of 396 to 360 B.C. This indicates that the ship was built sometime in the period 448 to 402 B.C. It foundered (sank) sometime between 396 and 360 B.C.

Great! These dates match up with the bracelet and earring found at the wreck – they were both from around 400 B.C.!

# LIFE IN ANCIENT GREECE

## The merchant's world

The City Museum's exhibition on life in ancient Greece is nearly complete. Dr. Jones and I are putting the finishing touches on the exhibition's web site. We decided to focus on 400 to 360 B.C., when our merchant sailed the seas.

Athens became the world's first democracy in the sixth century B.C. This new system of government soon spread to many of the other Greek city-states. Greek citizens (free men over the age of eighteen) voted in elections and participated in running the government. Women and slaves were not considered citizens and could not vote. Our seagoing merchant was probably a wealthy citizen who attended political meetings in his hometown. Chances are he was greatly missed when he didn't return from the sea.

The ancient Greeks loved science. They studied the planets, plants, animals, mathematics, and medicine. They were interested in geography, too, and greatly influenced cartography (mapmaking).

Olive oil and bread accompanied most meals in ancient Greece. I bought a bottle for my mom and dad.

Maybe the beautiful earrings were a gift from the merchant to his wife. Ancient Greek women had very little freedom and seldom left the house. Their job was to run the home and look after the children. The merchant's wife probably had a number of slaves to help her run the household.

Tuna, mackerel, and octopus were popular and readily available foods in ancient Greece.

## FOOD IN ANCIENT GREECE

**Everyone, rich or poor, drank wine in ancient Greece. They diluted it with water.**

In spite of the poor soil, ancient Greeks grew vegetables, such as lentils, beans, peas, onions, and garlic, and fruits, such as pomegranates, apples, pears, and figs. Herbs added flavor to foods, and honey was used as the main sweetener.

Lead fishing net weights found in the wreck indicate that the crew members probably fished to supplement their rations.

Goats grazed on the scrubby hillsides. The Greeks drank goat's milk and ate goat cheese.

## ANCIENT GREEK ALPHABET

| | |
|---|---|
| α | Alpha |
| β | Beta |
| γ | Gamma |
| δ | Delta |
| ε | Epsilon |
| ζ | Zeta |
| η | Eta |
| θ | Theta |
| ι | Iota |
| κ | Kappa |
| λ | Lambda |
| μ | Mu |
| ν | Nu |
| ξ | Xi |
| ο | Omicron |
| π | Pi |
| ρ | Rho |
| σ | Sigma |
| τ | Tau |
| υ | Upsilon |
| φ | Phi |
| χ | Chi |
| ψ | Psi |
| ω | Omega |

Phoenicians (who lived in the Middle East, where Lebanon and Syria are today) were the first to use an alphabet to keep records. Merchants brought the alphabet back to Greece, and its use soon spread throughout the Greek world.

Writing was mostly done on scrolls made from papyrus, an early type of paper made from reeds that grew in Egypt. Merchants brought papyrus paper back to Greece.

Our word "alphabet" comes from the names of the first two letters in the ancient Greek alphabet, <u>alpha</u> and <u>beta</u>.

From: Dr. Papadimas, the Museum, Crete
To: Alex Spencer, the City Museum
Subject: The crew of the merchant's ship

Dear Alex,
I want to report some new discoveries at the wreck site. In the bow (the front) of the ship, the divers found some plates, bowls, and oil jugs — four of each. I believe these belonged to the ship's crew, and if so, it means four men sailed on the ship: three crew members and the merchant (the captain). The design of the bowls and plates indicates they came from Athens — just like the silver coins. I think maybe the sailors were Athenian citizens. You see, Alex, treasure isn't just about gold and jewelry — everyday artifacts and the story they tell are just as valuable!

## Two years later

It's been two years since we discovered the wreck of the merchant's ship! I traveled back to Crete for my summer vacation. While I'm here, I decided to check in with Dr. Papadimas and his underwater excavation and research team.

Dr. Papadimas said his team raised every fragile piece of wood from the seabed and moved it to an old warehouse in Chania. Conservators soaked the huge timbers in freshwater for nearly eighteen months. Frequent water changes helped flush the seawater from the wood.

Next, the conservators injected the wood with polyethylene glycol (PEG), a special type of plastic-resin preservative. PEG stops the wood from shrinking and makes it solid again. Dr. Papadimas won't guarantee how long the ship will last, but without the PEG treatment, it would remain soft and spongy and soon disintegrate to dust.

Our wreck shows plenty of damage from shipworms. These saltwater worms burrow into shipwrecks and eat the wood.

Archaeologists recovered a number of weird-looking lumps from the wreck. Although seawater does not harm gold, it makes iron rust. As the iron corrodes, it reacts with the sand and other natural materials around it to form a stonelike encrusted clump called a concretion.

Rusty iron artifacts exposed to air disintegrate in minutes. In order to avoid destroying whatever was inside the concretions, the conservators x-rayed the lumps. I was amazed at the results. The X rays revealed the clear outlines of several spearheads!

**From: Alex Spencer**
**To: Dr. Helen Jones, the City Museum**
**Subject: Pirate attack!**

Dear Dr. Jones,
For the past two years, we thought the ship sank during a storm. But now Dr. Papadimas and the conservators think that the six iron spearheads indicate that the ship sank during a pirate attack! Fast-rowing boats full of pirates proved a constant threat to trading vessels around the Mediterranean. Dr. Papadimas believes that pirates captured the crew members, sold them into slavery, or perhaps even killed a few of the men. Pirates usually stole anything of value, especially easy-to-carry items. They hid evidence of their crime by sinking the ship. Pirates avoided detection and capture at all costs — in ancient Greece, the punishment for piracy was death by crucifixion! Fortunately for us, these pirates missed many of the ship's valuables.

USER 1
USER 2
USER 3

## A new ship

Dr. Papadimas invited me to visit a modern shipyard during my return trip to Crete to see an example of "experimental archaeology." I didn't know what that was, but when I arrived at the shipyard, he showed me a full-scale replica of the merchant's ship! It was created using tools, shipbuilding techniques, and materials as close as possible to those used by the ancient Greeks. Better yet, the ship will not just sit in a museum – Dr. Papadimas plans to take it on a voyage along the Greek coast!

I asked if he worried about the replica sinking, too. Dr. Papadimas said that "experimental archaeology" balances ancient knowledge and craftsmanship with modern technology and data – and guesswork! If the replica sinks, it isn't necessarily the fault of ancient technique or poor design. Instead, the archaeologists may have misinterpreted the data. As I walked around the replica, I imagined how proud the merchant felt when he saw this beautiful ship for the first time.

Like the original ship, the replica is constructed from pine.

In addition to its sail, four propulsion (rowing) oars – one for each of the crew members – power the ship. The two oars closer to the stern also steer the ship on its course.

Data collected during the excavation reveals the ship's dimensions – roughly 60 feet (18 m) by 13 feet (4 m). It carried about 28 tons (25 tonnes) of cargo. The replica is the same size.

The shipbuilding team covered all the wood with pine resin and melted fat. Linseed oil painted on the black portion of the hull helps make the ship water-resistant and protects its timbers from shipworm damage.

Dr. Papadimas studied ancient Greek boat paintings and consulted with modern boatbuilders and experienced sailors in order to design the ship's rigging and linen sail.

Linen fibers make up the natural cloth used for the sail. Linen comes from flax plants, which grow all around the Mediterranean Sea region. Linen cloth predates the use of sheep's wool for clothing.

**From: Dr. Helen Jones, the City Museum**
**To: Alex Spencer**
**Subject: Living the life of an ancient Greek sailor!**

Dear Alex,

I'm glad to hear that you saw the fantastic new replica ship! When it sets sail on the first voyage, we want to mimic as closely as possible the original conditions experienced by our ancient mariners. We hope that this experiment provides more information about the everyday experiences of ancient sailors.

We plan for a crew of three — trained in ancient sailing techniques — plus a captain to run the ship. The crew and captain will sleep out in the open, on top of the cargo, and go ashore to cook meals – just like the original sailors. The biggest difference between their voyage and ours is that one crew member is a woman — me!

USER 1
USER 2
USER 3

# LAUNCHING THE REPLICA

## A celebration

It's Easter weekend in Chania harbor, and the replica merchant's ship is about to set sail on its maiden (first) voyage. Greek merchants didn't go to sea during the winter months, so just like ancient sailors, our crew members waited until spring to take advantage of the best weather. Dr. Papadimas expects the voyage around the Greek islands to last two months. But like ancient Greek crews, our team members will sail at the mercy of the wind and the weather and cannot be sure of their exact arrival date. Likewise, Dr. Papadimas says that in order to keep the voyage as authentic as possible, his ship will sail without a radio or a lifeboat. To ensure the safety of the crew, however, a modern ship with communication and rescue equipment will escort the replica at all times.

Tonight, we dined on lamb kabobs (cooked on an open fire) and Greek salad (made with goat's cheese and olives). Starting tomorrow, the crew must survive on rations of olives, lentils, garlic, and any fish they can catch!

During several test runs, the replica reached speeds of 12 knots and rode 10-foot (3-m) waves with ease! A dingy transports crew members to the ship.

28

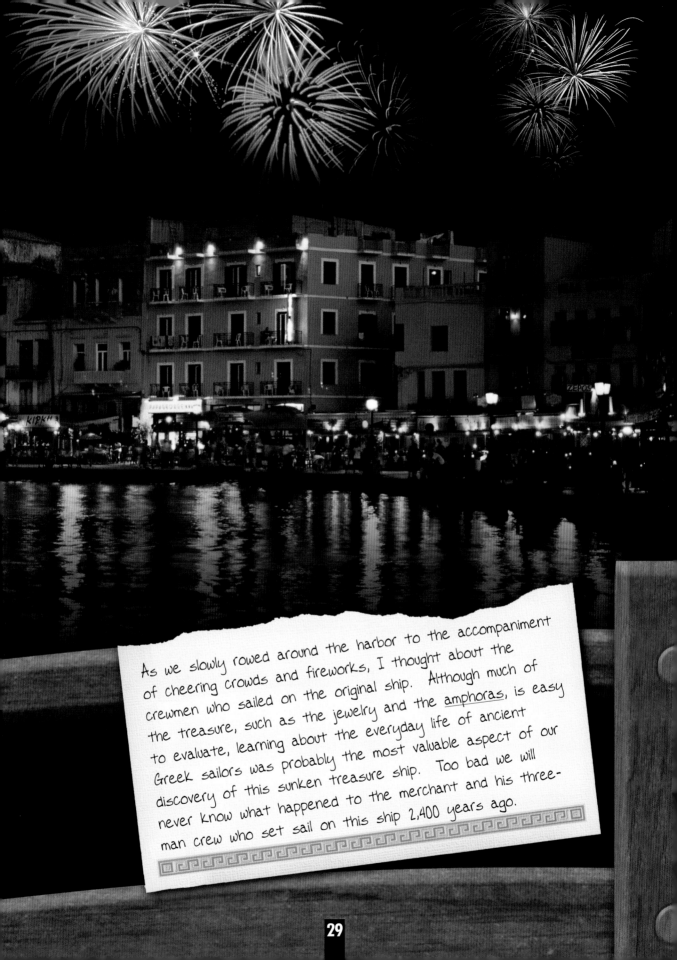

As we slowly rowed around the harbor to the accompaniment of cheering crowds and fireworks, I thought about the crewmen who sailed on the original ship. Although much of the treasure, such as the jewelry and the <u>amphoras</u>, is easy to evaluate, learning about the everyday life of ancient Greek sailors was probably the most valuable aspect of our discovery of this sunken treasure ship. Too bad we will never know what happened to the merchant and his three-man crew who set sail on this ship 2,400 years ago.

# GLOSSARY

**acropolis:** the upper part of a fortified section of a town that contained treasuries and temples, normally built on the highest hill.

*agora*: an open marketplace in ancient Greek towns.

**amphoras:** large, two-handled, clay storage jars with bulging bodies and narrow necks. They were sometimes decorated with paintings.

**amplify:** to enlarge in size or volume.

**antiquities:** ancient relics, artifacts, and monuments.

**archaeologist:** someone who studies the past by examining the physical remains left behind.

**architect:** someone who designs buildings and oversees their construction.

**artifacts:** objects made by humans, such as tools, pottery, or jewelry.

**auditorium:** the part of a theater in which the audience sits.

**authentic:** original; the true form of an item.

**cartography:** the science of making maps.

**caryatids:** a draped female figure that supports a horizontal portion of a building.

**citizen:** in ancient Greek city-states, a "free" male over the age of 18. Citizens were the only people allowed to vote.

**city-states:** an independent, self-governed area or "polis" of ancient Greece that included a main city and all the surrounding villages.

**colonies:** settlements in an outlying territory or country under the rule of their home country.

**concretion:** a hard, rocky mass formed from sand and other natural materials around corroded metals, such as iron.

**conservation:** the scientific process of cleaning, repairing, and preserving something.

**conservator:** a person who carries out conservation techniques, sometimes at a museum.

**corrode:** to wear away gradually by chemical action.

**crucifixion:** to affix someone's hands and feet to a cross until the person dies of suffocation.

**curator:** senior member of the staff of a museum, in charge of its collections.

**debris:** broken pieces of something; rubbish.

**democracy:** a system that allows ordinary people to participate in government.

**deteriorate:** to break down or degrade in quality.

**diadem:** a fancy headband.

**dilute:** to lessen the strength of something.

**disintegrate:** to decompose or fall apart.

**escort:** to travel along with for protection.

**excavate:** to dig for artifacts or fossils.

**experimental archaeology:** building a replica of an ancient building, vehicle, or machine using ancient technology.

**export:** to carry or send items out of one country for sale in another country.

**founder:** to sink or become disabled.

**frescoes:** water paintings on plaster.

**freshwater:** water that doesn't contain salt.

**frieze:** a sculptured or ornamental band on a building or a piece of furniture.

**fund-raiser:** someone who raises money, usually to benefit a particular cause or project.

**hoplites:** ancient Greek foot soldiers who wore heavy helmets and carried spears and large, round shields.

**import:** to bring something in from another country.

**labyrinth:** a mazelike network of passageways or tunnels with many dead ends.

**lentils:** vegetables, such as peas and beans.

**linen:** a cloth made from flax fibers.

**marine:** relating to the oceans and saltwater.

**mint:** the process of making coins.

**Murex:** a type of sea snail used for making dye.

**myth:** a traditional story that includes popular beliefs or explains a practice or natural phenomena.

**navigate:** to direct the course of a ship.

**oracle:** a place where ancient gods spoke to the people; also, the person who was perceived as a message-bearer of the gods.

**papyrus:** paper made from a reedlike plant that grew near the Nile River.

**polyethylene glycol (PEG):** a chemical used to conserve waterlogged wood.

**PVC:** polyvinyl chloride, a type of plastic often used for tubes, piping, and as electrical insulation.

**Pythia:** the high priestess at the Delphi oracle.

**radiocarbon-dating:** a method of dating items, such as bone or wood, that were once living, by measuring the amount of carbon-14 left inside.

**replica:** an accurate model.

**resin:** hard, rubbery plant juice or plastic.

**rhyton:** a drinking vessel shaped like an animal head.

**rigging:** the ropes used on a ship for controlling the sails and supporting the mast.

**salvage:** to recover a ship and its cargo from the sea.

**scuba diver:** a person who swims underwater using SCUBA (**S**elf-**C**ontained **U**nderwater **B**reathing **A**pparatus).

**shipworms:** marine worms that burrow into and eat submerged wood.

**smuggling:** illegally importing or exporting goods.

**symposiums:** drinking and talking parties held for and attended only by ancient Greek men.

**tunic:** a plain garment with or without sleeves (often worn belted) and worn by both men and women.

**vessel:** another word for a ship or boat; also, a container that holds a liquid.

**X rays:** photographs taken with invisible radiation.

# MORE INFORMATION

## BOOKS

*Ancient Shipwrecks.*  K. C. Smith  (Franklin Watts)

*Atlas of Shipwrecks and Treasures.*  Nigel Pickford (DK)

*Buried Treasures of the Atlantic Coast:  Legends of Sunken Pirate Treasures, Mysterious Caches, and Jinxed Ships — Maine to Florida.  Buried Treasures* (series).  W. C. Jameson (August House)

*The Children's Atlas of Lost Treasures.  The Children's Atlas* (series).  Struan Reid (Millbrook)

*The Search for Sunken Treasure:  Exploring the World's Great Shipwrecks.*  Robert F. Marx (Key Porter Books)

*Underwater Archaeology:  Exploring the World Beneath the Sea.  Discoveries* (series).  Jean-Yves Blot (Harry N. Abrams)

## WEB SITES

www.brainpop.com/tech/transportation/submarines
  Learn how a submarine works.

www.cyberpursuits.com/archeo/uw-arch.asp
  Lists links to underwater archaeology web sites.

www.jason.org/expeditions/jason7/
  Check out the real-life expeditions for students.

www.unknowncountry.com/news/?id=1119
  Read about an underwater temple in the Mediterranean.

## VIDEOS

*Atocha:  Quest For Treasure.*  (National Geographic)

*Great Cities of the Ancient World — Athens & Ancient Greece.*  (Questar)

# INDEX